CAPRICORN

CAPRICORN

Let your Sun sign show you the way
to a happy and fulfilling life

Marion Williamson & Pam Carruthers

ARCTURUS

ARCTURUS

This edition published in 2021 by Arcturus Publishing
Limited
26/27 Bickels Yard, 151–153 Bermondsey Street,
London SE1 3HA

ISBN: 978-1-83940-148-0
AD008770UK

Printed in China

CONTENTS

Introduction

*W*elcome, Capricorn! You have just taken a step towards what might become a lifelong passion. When astrology gets under your skin, there's no going back. Astrology helps you understand yourself and the people around you, and its dazzling insights become more fascinating the deeper you go.

Just as the first humans turned to the life-giving Sun for sustenance and guidance, your astrological journey begins with your Sun sign of Capricorn. First, we delve deeply into the heart of what makes you tick, then we'll continue to unlock your cosmic potential by exploring love, your career and health, where you might prefer to live, and how you get along with family and friends.

Then it's over to gifted astrologer, Pam Carruthers, for her phenomenal birthdate analysis where she reveals personality insights for every single specific Capricorn birthday.

In the last part of the book we get right inside how astrology works by revealing the different layers that will help you understand your own birth chart and offer the planetary tools to get you started.

Are you ready, Capricorn? Let's find out why you're the zodiac's highest achiever …

CUSP DATES FOR CAPRICORN
22 December – 20 January

The exact time of the Sun's entry into each zodiac sign varies every year, so it's impossible to list them all. If you were born a day either side of the dates above, you're a 'cusp' baby. This means you may feel like you're a blend of Capricorn/Sagittarius or Capricorn/Aquarius, or you may instinctively just know that you're one sign right to your core.

Going deeper

If you want to know once and for all whether you're a Sagittarius, Capricorn or Aquarius, you can look up your birthdate in a planetary ephemeris, of which there are plenty online. (See page 102 for more information.) This shows the exact moment the Sun moved into a new zodiac sign for the month you were born.

The Capricorn personality

*Y*ou are a realistic, practical and hard-working person – the most ambitious character in the zodiac. The astrological symbol for Capricorn is the Goat, sometimes depicted as a mythical sea goat. The Goat represents your patient determination to scale great heights and reach the pinnacle in all your endeavours. You have lofty goals and both the intelligence and diligence to achieve them. As an Earth sign you are pragmatic and stoical, firmly rooted in the tangible world, and you trust in what you can see, touch and build. Responsible, structure-loving Saturn is your ruling planet, which gives you a realistic, if slightly cynical, outlook on life. You expect to work very hard to achieve success and respect others who have set a good example.

OLD HEAD, YOUNG SHOULDERS

Capricorns tend to start life with an old head on young shoulders and lighten up as they age. Stern Saturn often presents Capricorns with challenges early in life and you may have had to shoulder extra responsibilities, or encountered limiting circumstances. The humbler your beginnings, the greater your determination to overcome any challenges on the rocky road up the mountain. And in dealing with character-forming situations so young, you learned to become self-reliant. You are confident in your ability to succeed, but Saturn probably left you with a few niggly self-esteem issues, or a feeling of insecurity, which you'll be determined to mask by flinging yourself into a constant state of refinement and improvement.

On top of setting your sights very high in your career, you're also something of a social climber, and enjoy rubbing shoulders with people who've 'made it' in your eyes. Some will be dear friends, but you're probably guilty of indulging in a spot of name-dropping, hoping you'll appear a little more impressive into the bargain. You're not a loud or ostentatious person, but you want to be respected for your achievements, because secretly you may feel like you're an imposter who just got lucky.

You're not always the fastest to learn new skills but you have legendary stamina and patience. Where others give up when the going gets rough, you keep on slowly but surely ploughing through until you have what you want in your sights. Your burdens become lighter as you get older – or perhaps it's your attitude that changes, as you learn not to be so hard on yourself. Saturn has set you an intimidating set of standards to live by, but he has also endowed you with the organisational skills, prudence and self-discipline to shine. As you gain confidence you brighten with every achievement, mellowing with age as a cheerier more carefree you emerges over time.

CLEVER WITH MONEY

As a sensible, accumulative Earth sign, you're excellent with money. You're not a frivolous spender. With a mature head on your shoulders you're not about to waste the money you put so much time and energy into creating. One of the main reasons you're such a financial whizz is that you know when to act. You don't procrastinate, and you don't make excuses – you have a plan and you stick to it. It might not be rocket science, but surprisingly few people have the common sense or discipline to plough through tasks in quite the same way.

You're a saver and a prudent investor, clever at maths, facts and figures – and careers in finance will be an attractive option. You're a cool operator and a thoughtful strategist and if you don't know how something works, you'll learn! Not impulsive by nature, you spend your money wisely, and you can spot the value in other people's skills and talents. With an eye for the things that stand the test of time, Capricorns make excellent art and antique dealers, estate agents and jewellers. Yours isn't a boom or bust zodiac sign and you'll make your fortune slowly, over a long period of time. Even financially embarrassed Capricorns will have a business plan or two carefully tucked away, waiting for the right moment.

SIMPLY THE BEST

Although cautious with money, when you feel secure enough, you'll wish to show the world that you've made it – or are at least on your way there! You have excellent taste and want to look and sound like you mean business. A traditionalist at heart, you have something of a formal manner and conservative appearance. Dressed to impress in darker colours, timeless designer suits and tasteful accessories, you're usually impeccably presented, with neat hair and an imposing air of sophistication. Unless you have plenty of outgoing, brash Fire or Air signs in your birth chart, you'll rarely be seen in scruffy or outlandish clothes. Your appreciation for history is reflected in your passion for well-preserved vintage pieces, and you'd rather sport a fine antique watch or ring than anything too tasteless or contemporary.

You like old-money style in fashion, furnishings and the arts, leaning towards classical music and opera rather than jazz or pop, and you'll swoon at the ballet, rather than stage dive into a rock concert mosh pit. Your appreciation of history and time has you in awe, and you'll love to spend rainy afternoons gazing at the old masters in celebrated art galleries and wondering at the remains of ancient civilization in world-renowned museums. As a lover of the great outdoors, a typical Capricorn would be coated head to toe in old-fashioned but expensive country clobber, and drive around their substantial estate in a Range Rover.

LONELY AT THE TOP

Authoritative Saturn ensures you feel comfortable at the helm in any business. Your drive, knowledge and sheer hard work eventually propel you to the top of your game and, as you've been headed up that mountain most of your life, it's naturally where you feel most confident and secure. Whether you find yourself as a CEO, the head of a small company or as a self-made entrepreneur, you are happy being the person accountable for making all the important, or final, decisions.

Not everyone wishes to be tethered to their job, or cares as much about their public persona, and it can get lonely up there. You'll have made many acquaintances and enjoy a plethora of colleagues and co-workers, so romance may have taken something of a back seat while you concentrated on your career. But family is extremely important to you and you have a strong sense of duty. You wouldn't hesitate to give up your career completely if you had to look after an elderly parent, and your loyalty to your roots would see you stick with a family business to make it a success, even if you'd secretly have preferred to try something different.

FUNNY FEELINGS

Nobody could accuse you of coming across as too gushy! Capricorns usually have tight reign over their emotions or are uncomfortable expressing their more complicated feelings. For all your polished exterior, you're not quite as at ease with your inner world but, again, you tend to form an easier relationship with your emotions as you get older. If you don't have many Fire or Water signs in your birth chart, having a Saturn Sun sign can make you more apt to analyse your thoughts or feelings instead of allowing yourself to feel sad, angry, jealous or even joyful.

As you are such a perfectionist, you should guard against becoming so caught up in chasing a particular dream or ambition to the exclusion of everything else, because if things don't work out as planned, Saturn can make you be very hard on yourself. It's vitally important you don't get sucked into a negative spiral, as you'll probably dwell far too long on what you could have done to improve things – even if it no longer matters. Use pragmatic Saturn to your advantage, to allow yourself to see that you did your best – and employ your wonderfully dry sense of humour to help you loosen up a little and enjoy life to its fullest.

CANCER LESSON

Opposite signs of the zodiac, Cancer and Capricorn represent the polarity between having a home life as your epicentre – or a successful professional career. You share many similarities with each other, as well as contrasting differences. You are both sentimental creatures, though neither of you like to display your emotions too freely in public. You both are shrewd with money, share a love of tradition, and value a secure and structured home life. Cancer understands why Capricorns may appear aloof, because they can see past any social armour to the real, less confident, person inside. Cancer empathises, as they too are tougher in the outside world than they are when they're relaxing with loved ones. Deep down, Capricorn wants to be loved, and Cancer's lesson is that a balance between being too work-oriented, and having a loving partner or home life is entirely possible. Saturn-ruled people often fear rejection or abandonment, and Cancer teaches that being open to love doesn't necessarily make you vulnerable.

Capricorn
Motto

I'LL QUIETLY BEND
THAT LEARNING
CURVE INTO A
STRAIGHT LINE
THAT'S POINTING
TO SUCCESS.

Capricorn in love

*N*obody can accuse you of wearing rose-tinted spectacles when it comes to love and romance. As one of the most practical Earth signs in the zodiac, you're not about to leap up and down proclaiming your affections from the rooftops. At least not until you've thoroughly checked their reputation and background on social media, found out if they have a car, and what their future plans involve. You do have a slightly unfair reputation for being too status-conscious when it comes to choosing a partner, but that's just because you know there's no point in being with someone who doesn't share similar aspirations.

It's not that you don't want to be in love, it's just that you're the least likely sign of the zodiac to be blinded by it. You long to meet someone you can cherish and share your life with, and as you're deeply attractive, wise, funny and refined – you won't have trouble attracting the real thing. But Saturn made you a realist, and he probably taught you quite early on in life to keep your true feelings private until you are quite sure it's safe to reveal them – and this can take time. You may even put off looking for a relationship until you're happy that your career is on the right track, as you're wise enough to consider how much time you would be able to commit to a serious relationship when you're still trying to establish yourself in your chosen field. When you do meet someone suitable, you don't treat it lightly because you know it could be a lifetime's commitment. You'll take things seriously, calmly and quite slowly, so that you can be sure they can be trusted with your surprisingly fragile heart. Then when you do commit, you're all in – mind, body and soul. When you trust another enough to let your guard down, they'll be delighted to see a side of you that the rest of the word rarely does – loving, gentle, and passionate – with a wickedly deadpan sense of humour.

EVERYTHING'S PERFECT

Your Saturn work ethic also applies to relationships. You don't expect even the most wonderful love affairs to be sunshine and rainbows. You understand that nobody is perfect, and you'll include your own flaws and idiosyncrasies in that equation. The best partnerships take effort and, unless you have a predominance of flighty Air or reckless Fire signs in your chart, you will be devoted to making the commitment work. Naturally you'll enjoy setting goals for yourself as a couple – perhaps even working hard to set up a business together.

A traditionalist at heart, you'll likely adopt the conventional model for love and romance and apply your high Capricorn standards. You'll choose a stable, albeit rather formal approach with engagement, setting up an impressive home together – and children will be discussed at the appropriate time. Your relationship may appear a little austere to people who don't know you, but your friends and loved ones will see a completely different side. Although always keen to project a grandiose vision of your life together, when it's just you two – you drop the stiff formalities and allow yourself to be playful and vulnerable.

TRICKY EMOTIONS

The initial exciting stages of romance can be a little overwhelming for your usual cool, calm and collected persona, and you're actually far more comfortable when things settle down. Though this can be a tougher time for your partner, who may feel concerned that you're withdrawing your more spontaneous emotions. This is probably not a conscious decision and is just a sign that you're relaxed enough to be yourself. But you can't expect your partner to be psychic, so try not to let your practical side override or obscure your fun-loving, affectionate nature. Your ruler Saturn may be something of a 'glass half empty' type of ruling planet, but you could do well to remember that once the hard work is done – you're allowed to enjoy yourself!

Most compatible love signs

Cancer – you share important values with your opposite sign, Cancer. You're both conscientious, cautious and can make heaps of money together.

Scorpio – you're both quite reticent to show how you really feel, but there are fireworks when you do!

Taurus – loyal, steady and determined, you feel safe with Taurus, and these comfort-loving characters will help you to relax and smell the flowers along the way.

Least compatible love signs

Sagittarius – you're quite suspicious of anyone who seems recklessly jolly for no apparent reason.

Aries – they're quite attractive for a while with their big ideas and passions, but they don't have the stamina or vision to back up anything they say.

Gemini – you like tradition, Gemini is faddish, you have serious life goals ... they're all chit chat ... you don't have time for this!

Capricorn at work

You are a born business mastermind – the hardest worker in the zodiac – and if you haven't already achieved something prestigious or impressive, you'll be slowly working your way towards it. After all, reaching the top is what goat-people naturally want to do. You size up any challenges in your way with a cool head, and learn the skills you need on the steep slope to the top of the mountain.

You're super-practical and organised, and will probably have a strict plan of action. As one of the most disciplined people around, you can be a little harsh on yourself if you feel you've wasted an opportunity, or spent too much time on something frivolous, like consuming a meal in your lunch hour ... or having a loo break.

EMPLOYEE OF THE YEAR

As an employee, you're the first person to switch the light on in the office and are often the last to leave. You're trusted with extra heavy workloads because you're known as a steady pair of hands, methodical, conscientious and reliable. You don't quibble, and you'll never tell your boss that something can't be done

– you'll find a way even if it means working overtime or learning a whole new set of skills.

You always have half an eye on the top job, but totally respect the hard work and solid effort it takes to get there. As a disciplined Saturn-ruled person, you wouldn't feel comfortable in a position you felt was handed to you on a plate. You need to feel you've earned your right to be there.

You're generally the quiet, conservatively dressed, well-spoken person who's careful with money. You can be trusted to look after anything from the kitty for the tea and biscuits, to the economy of a large country. You're that rare breed that's gifted at maths and enjoys accounts, so you find working out the company tax bill quite satisfying and even feel a twinge of pleasure in paying them.

Where other zodiac signs would shrug it off pretty fast, if you make a mistake at work you'll feel miserable, as so much of your self-esteem is wrapped up with your job. But for the same reason, you'll learn from every misstep, and vow never to make the same error twice.

You have the drive and ambition to be a self-made entrepreneur as you're not easily discouraged, and your decision to set up your own business will be based on facts, and meticulous research. You also have the patience and appreciation of structure to draw you to a career in accountancy or working in a bank. Goal-oriented, you would enjoy setting regular targets for anyone in your team, whether you work for a large corporation or a small niche business.

GOAT AT THE TOP

If you're a Capricorn boss – you're right where you ought to be! A high achiever, you belong to the corporate world, and your patience and exceptional problem-solving skills mean you have the potential to be one of the most efficient and committed professionals in the workforce. You favour traditional methods and are a bit suspicious of shortcuts. Saturn may make you feel weighed down with responsibility, and you're generally quiet about your considerable achievements. However, you will allow yourself a few aspirational status symbols – a sedate but expensive company car or an imposing desk or office.

Firm but fair, you're a decent boss, who rewards loyalty, and a job well done, but if anyone tries to pull the wool over your eyes you'll not be amused. People need to be honest, put in the hours and, above all, show you the same respect you'd have for a person in your position. Although you're the ultimate professional, and can be a little shy or formal, when you feel comfortable, your cynical, dry sense of humour comes out to play, surprising anyone who doesn't know you well. But you have to earn that rare privilege with a Capricorn boss.

Most compatible colleagues

Gemini – they talk too much, and their silly sense of humour is at odds with your dry wit, but they've got the sparky ideas and creativity that balance out your practical, methodical approach.

Pisces – like you, Pisces prefers to work quietly in the background, and you value their vision and imagination when working on projects together.

Virgo – these practical, organised, conscientious characters are the zodiac's favourite worker bee, and the pair of you are an ambitious, sensible powerhouse.

Least compatible colleagues

Capricorn – two Capricorns together either come to a complete standstill or are ruthlessly competitive.

Leo – Leo needs to be reminded how good they are at everything which, as a self-disciplined Saturnian type, just gets on your goat!

Aquarius – you rarely feel like you're on the same page with Aquarius, but that's because you're not – and neither is anyone else!

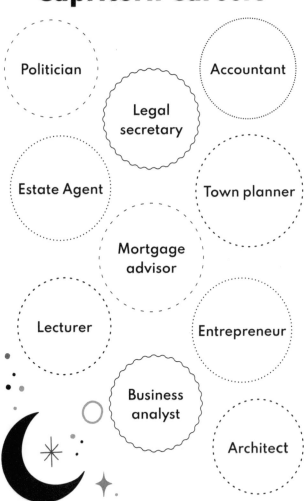

Perfect
Capricorn Careers

Politician

Legal secretary

Accountant

Estate Agent

Town planner

Mortgage advisor

Lecturer

Entrepreneur

Business analyst

Architect

Capricorn
Work Ethic

IF AT FIRST YOU
DON'T SUCCEED,
THEN YOU SHOULD
HAVE DONE IT THE
WAY I TOLD YOU
TO IN THE FIRST
PLACE.

Capricorn friends and family

*Y*ou're a loyal friend, reliable and constant, and you see it as your duty to look after the people who have been in your life for a long time. Old friends feel like family to you, and with sage-old Saturn, the Lord of Time, as your ruling planet, you'll naturally get on with people from different generations. You're a realist at heart and fully accept that you won't be young forever, which gives you an unusually deep respect for older people's knowledge and wisdom.

You also appreciate having a good old-fashioned moan with friends, sharing your work woes, having a gripe about the government and generally lamenting the state of the world with someone who agrees with you. You're a very therapeutic person in this respect, as everyone needs a friend who they can have a jolly good grumble with and set the world to rights.

DEADPAN HUMOUR

You also deeply appreciate people who can bring you out of a gloomy mood, or who can make you forget about work entirely. Your ruler Saturn might not be the cheeriest of planets, but he's taught you to enjoy a healthy dose of well-observed sarcasm. You'll have at least one friend with a droll sense of humour and the pair of you will probably have your own secret language and keep each other in stitches.

You are extremely self-reliant and trust yourself first and foremost – so it can be tough sharing any fears or personal problems with others. You rarely admit to any insecurities and are a bit worried that others will think you unworthy of your success, but usually the opposite is true. When you let friends and loved ones in, you'll discover that rather than judging you, they'll be touched that you let down your guard to reveal your true self. When you feel that the real you is valued and accepted, warts and all, you will feel much lighter and less pessimistic.

A good old-fashioned night out on the town, watching a stand-up comedian, or an evening at the movies with friends, will all give you a break from being the one in charge. It will make you realise that the world keeps on turning, even if you're not there to supervise.

CAPRICORN AT HOME

Always striving to attain the best life can offer, regardless of your own background or family circumstances, you want the best for your loved ones, so you're usually the person in charge at home, as well as in the office. Whether you have your own family or not, you'll work hard to secure a home base where you can shed the weight of the world from your shoulders and relax. Tasteful, but slightly austere, your home ambience reflects your deep sense of connection with the past. Grandiose antique furniture, elegant bookcases, classical décor and cool retro pieces reflect your excellent and refined taste.

CAPRICORN PARENT

You want respect from your children and have an authoritative, slightly aloof manner. You'll encourage any talents or skills from an early age and will happily support any musical or creative interests. Having fun with your kids is vitally important so that your offspring see your lighter side, as well as the serious career-oriented person.

CAPRICORN CHILD

Capricorn kids often seem older than their years and need to learn to relax and be curious about their world. These earnest boys and girls crave approval and should be praised for just being themselves, as well as being encouraged for their achievements.

Healthy Capricorn

*Y*ou're blessed with a robust constitution and have the self-discipline to stick to an exercise regime that gets you the results you want. Even the most intimidating fitness challenges don't scare you off, as long as you have the space and time to work incrementally towards mastering your goal. As Capricorn is the sign of the Goat, climbing will be an obvious activity choice, but any form of exercise where you steadily work towards success works best. You have the stamina for long distance running and have the grace and poise to be an elegant ice skater or gymnast. If you're very shy, as some Capricorns tend to be, attending a regular gym class with others means you'll break through some anxieties as well as toning up your body.

FOOD AND DRINK

You have bags of Saturnian self-control when it comes to food and nutrition and find it easier than most to adapt to healthy eating habits. When you're in the zone, you eat regularly, stick to nutritious options, and you don't find it too hard to cut back on calories if you need to. But if you're overworking, food can get forgotten and you'll find yourself relying on 24-hour takeaways or living on caffeine and high-energy drinks. This might inject you with the temporary burst of energy you need to complete your tax return, but eventually you'll burn out and feel even more exhausted in the long run. Getting plenty of rest is crucial for stressed-out Capricorns, as lack of downtime can see you lying awake at night thinking about your work, when you ought to be fast asleep.

BEING KIND TO YOURSELF

You want to be the best at whatever you are doing, and Saturn can be a hard taskmaster. But beware that you are not pushing yourself too far with exercise, as overdoing it can put pressure on your bones – which can be a weak point. If you're going through a particularly busy or difficult time at work, you might neglect your gym membership or not have time to exercise at all. But getting enough fresh air, natural daylight and feeling connected with the ground, is vital for Earth signs to stay healthy and vibrant. A decent brisk walk every day should keep you ticking over if that's all you have time for.

Sleep is critical and meditation and relaxation methods will help you unwind and focus on something other than work. You, more than anyone else, need to actively make time to be kind to yourself, as you find it easy to self-critical if you feel you're not getting enough done, or feel dissatisfied with your efforts. When you appreciate yourself a little more, you'll find that you're actually one of the few zodiac signs who looks healthier as they age – and the sign most likely to enjoy a sprightly retirement.

BODY AREA: BONES, KNEES AND SKIN

Capricorns are said to have beautiful legs and fine bone structure. As the sign that carries the weight of responsibility, this can be tough on your bones – and most Capricorns have an alarming story or two to tell about their knees or teeth.

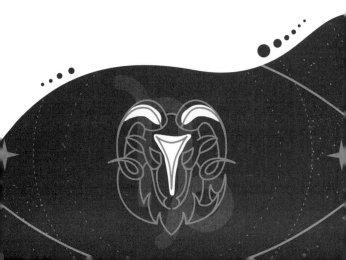

Capricorn on the move

When you have decided where you want to go, you'll set money aside for your trip or will diligently save for your break away for months in advance. You like to do things properly, and in style – no spontaneous backpacking for you! You think it through carefully and plan what to visit. As the zodiac's workaholic, you're rarely not thinking about your job and often conversations with people you meet on your trips turn out to be valued business contacts. Often your reason for visiting a particular place will be because you think it will inspire your next big business idea, or you'll choose somewhere you'd like to check out as a future home.

GET PACKING

Cautious and grounded, you'll make sure you have a quality travel insurance package in place. You're a bit of a worrier, and will pack accordingly, with a secure money belt, a large First Aid kit, insect repellent, sensible walking shoes, plenty of sunscreen and a few home comforts to help you settle in.

Leaving home can make the rooted Capricorn a little nervous, especially as it means leaving the office.

You may worry that your work will pile up, or that a colleague could ruin a carefully planned project. The anxiety of leaving work behind can colour your vacation planning, and you'll have read up on all the possible dangers you may encounter on your travels. You will expect to encounter a few thieves and scoundrels along the way, or at least will have discovered which areas it's best to avoid. You take the conventional route when travelling and have rather old-fashioned expensive taste. You'd rather stay in an established hotel with a good reputation than anywhere too fresh and funky – and you're often very loyal, visiting favourite establishments over and over again.

ON THE ROAD

Once you're on the road, and are sufficiently distracted from work, you're a cautious but curious travelling companion. You're always prepared for a crisis, and can produce a sticking plaster, safety pin, or mosquito swatter at a moment's notice. You have an unfair reputation as being stingy with your cash, but it's simply not true. You're actually one of the most likely zodiac signs to spend good money on quality accommodation and travel, but you'll not splash out on trinkets or souvenirs – and you'll be suspicious of anyone giving you a hard sell.

You're an excellent map reader and will be very knowledgeable about the places you visit – sometimes to a gleefully annoying extent! You'll enjoy having company on your trip but, like most Earth signs, you dislike being rushed. You'll have a schedule and you'll cross things off your list, and whether travelling with friends or family, you'll expect everyone to obediently stick to your plan.

YOUR KIND OF PLACE

You have a deep sense of reverence for the past, so historical tours, museums and places steeped in intriguing traditions, fill you with pleasure. Athens, Jerusalem and Alexandria will captivate your imagination as you delve into the former glory of these ancient civilisations. And classically elegant cities such as St Petersburg, Prague, Vienna and Florence will impress you with their rich cultural heritage, extravagant restaurants, opulent buildings, and sophisticated nightlife.

As an Earth sign, beautiful nature will always have the power to move you, and sweeping open skies, lakes, and your favourite natural sight − mountains − may even be impressive enough to take your mind off your career for a while. Extraordinary places such as Cusco in Peru, the capital of the Inca empire, or the majestic Kirkjufell mountain in Iceland will captivate your heart and soothe your soul.

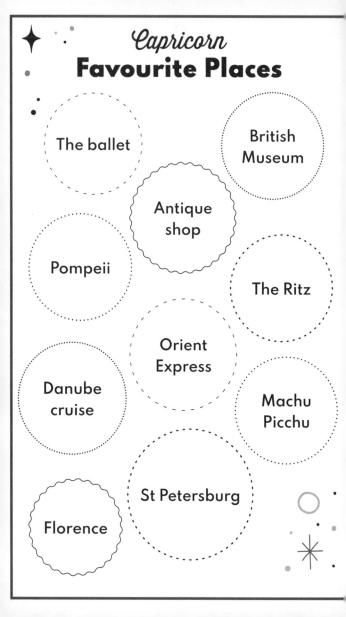

Capricorn
Favourite Places

The ballet

British Museum

Antique shop

Pompeii

The Ritz

Orient Express

Danube cruise

Machu Picchu

St Petersburg

Florence

Capricorn
Travel Ethic

YOU CALL IT
A RUIN, I CALL
IT MY NEXT
DESTINATION.

Capricorn
BIRTHDATE
PERSONALITIES

Discover your
personal forecast
for the day of
your birth.

22 December

*Y*ou are a sensitive and strong person with a tough exterior but a marshmallow-soft inner centre. You are capable of immense self-control and are the ultimate professional, totally dedicated to your career and able to work long hours to achieve that coveted promotion. Your heart is tender, and you can be quite soppy, easily bursting into tears when stories of orphaned children appear on the news. You are not one to blow your own trumpet and your charitable work is done quietly with no fuss. You are a superb manager and people feel that you listen to their concerns, so you would excel in Human Resources. Marriage is almost essential as you need a partner to feel complete. A family get-together is your idea of happiness, and you're the perfect person to make it happen.

STRENGTHS
Modest, committed

WEAKNESSES
Tendency to overwork,
sentimental

MEDITATION
*When one door closes,
another door opens.*

23 December

*Y*ou are an assertive and purposeful person with high ambitions and deep desire for recognition. With a strong belief in yourself and a willingness to work very hard, you have the abilities of a natural leader. You can't bear to be in a subordinate position, but luckily for you, people generally agree that you are right person to be in charge. Once in the right position, you lead with your heart and radiate warmth. You achieve superb results because of the care and preparation that you put into your projects. Be aware of a tendency to let power to go to your head – you can turn into a dictator and lord it over people! In relationships, your partner has to be your equal and yet mustn't outshine you or you will not flourish. Your creativity needs an outlet, and singing for the fun of it is a natural talent.

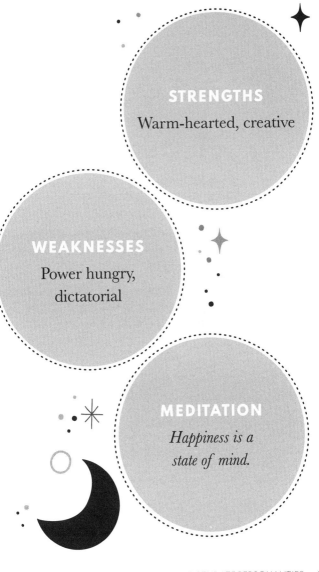

STRENGTHS
Warm-hearted, creative

WEAKNESSES
Power hungry,
dictatorial

MEDITATION
*Happiness is a
state of mind.*

24 December

Y ou are a modest yet highly successful person who enjoys helping others. Highly skilled, you pride yourself on the professionalism of your work. You are not known for being showy, and prefer to keep behind the scenes as you are quite shy. You are interested in diet and nutrition so you can do well in the health industry. You excel at streamlining systems and finding the most efficient methods. However, you tend to find fault in everything as you have very high standards. With friends you can relax and have a wicked sense of humour. In relationships you are content to settle down early as you love caring for people, and a family brings you great joy. Decluttering and reorganizing your home is one of the most enjoyable things you can do in your spare time.

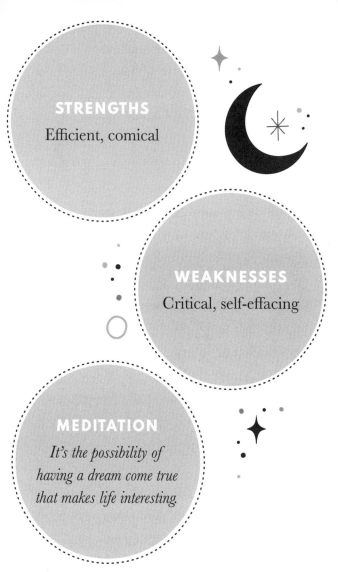

STRENGTHS
Efficient, comical

WEAKNESSES
Critical, self-effacing

MEDITATION
It's the possibility of having a dream come true that makes life interesting.

25 December

You are a charming and well-mannered person who knows the rules of etiquette and abides by them. Although you have a love of tradition, you can be progressive in your views. You have an innate sense of justice and your words – though always polite – are powerful when directed to upholding the truth. Entering the legal profession as an advocate, or following a career as a foreign diplomat, are both attractive paths for you. A weakness is your indecision and you can sit on the fence for a long time. Your relationship is a true partnership and you seek an ally – a partner who shares your ambitions. You are loyal and tender, and thrive on entertaining your mutual business contacts. Obsessed with looking good, you need to be stylish even when you exercise, so tennis or cricket has great appeal.

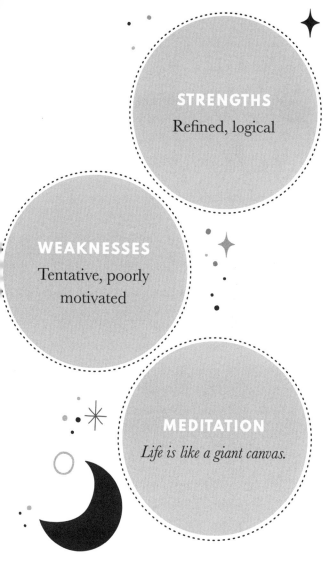

STRENGTHS
Refined, logical

WEAKNESSES
Tentative, poorly motivated

MEDITATION
Life is like a giant canvas.

26 December

*Y*ou are a charismatic and dedicated person with huge powers of endurance. Whatever you start you finish and you are able to confront tremendous obstacles and challenges. Physically and emotionally strong, you take pride in keeping yourself in good shape and keep improving your qualifications. As a leader you are strong and decisive so you are suited to a position of responsibility. However, you can be too tough and unable to see that others can't keep up with you. When you apply your powerful will towards helping the underdog you come into your own. You have traditional values so marriage is for keeps and you will make every effort to ensure it works. You can be too serious and austere so your downtime needs to be fun. You enjoy thrills so an exciting ride at a theme park could do the trick.

STRENGTHS
Emotionally strong,
a good leader

WEAKNESSES
Severe in manner,
exacting

MEDITATION
*Without hard work,
nothing grows but weeds.*

27 December

You are an enthusiastic and dedicated person with a great sense of adventure. You are fearless and have few concerns about the future as you have faith in your abilities and are willing to put in a lot of effort to achieve your dreams. You speculate to accumulate and your confidence and dignity ensures that people value and look up to you. You adore travel and have a broad outlook on life. Once wealthy you donate to worthy causes. Although you are a consummate professional, you love playing practical jokes on people – much to their annoyance. When young, your relationships are free and easy and you can be quite cavalier with your affections. As you mature you begin to appreciate your need for a partner who is also your best friend. Your favourite way to relax is walking or hill climbing.

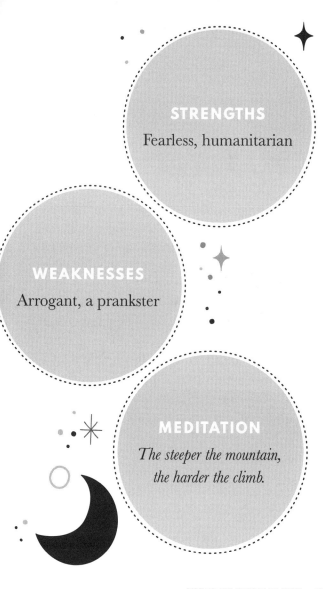

STRENGTHS
Fearless, humanitarian

WEAKNESSES
Arrogant, a prankster

MEDITATION
*The steeper the mountain,
the harder the climb.*

28 December

*Y*ou are a sophisticated and practical person who aims high in life and usually succeeds. You have a huge amount of common sense and a quiet charm that grows on people. Steadfast and dependable, you can be too serious and so focused on self-advancement that you don't stop to smell the roses. You are the backbone of any organization you care to work for, but you have your eyes set on the top job. You love old things and appreciate craftsmanship and will pay top dollar for quality. Cheap stuff just doesn't do it for you. You approach relationships cautiously and take time to evaluate the merits of potential partners. Once committed you are a sensual lover with a witty sense of humour. Purposeless fun is much needed in your life – playing kids games would do it.

STRENGTHS
Refined, witty

WEAKNESSES
Serious, self-absorbed

MEDITATION
Stay young – carry your childhood with you.

29 December

*Y*ou are an eccentric person with a highly original way of doing things. Highly intelligent, your mental powers can verge on genius. You are quick to take on new concepts. Concerned with promoting a cause, you are attracted to local politics and actively serving your community. Having space and freedom is crucial for your well-being and being tied to a routine job is an anathema. Being self-employed and running your own enterprise is far more in keeping with your style. At times you are rather cool and distant and people can think you're ignoring them. In relationships you tend to take your time and seek a partner who'll be a friend, be materially successful, and keep you on your toes. Social activities that involve some fun, such as line dancing, are entertaining and good relaxation for you.

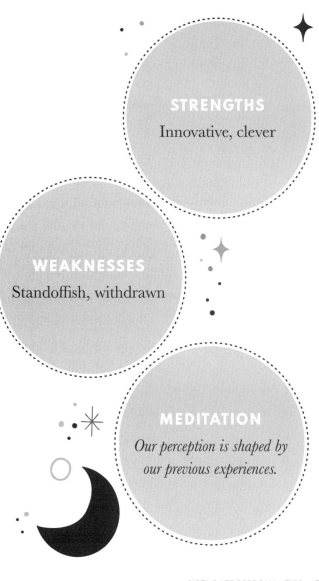

STRENGTHS

Innovative, clever

WEAKNESSES

Standoffish, withdrawn

MEDITATION

Our perception is shaped by our previous experiences.

30 December

*Y*ou are a disciplined and sombre person, yet have a youthful air about you. You impress people with your mental agility and logical, well-considered arguments. Light-hearted but never superficial, what you say is taken seriously. You have an extensive vocabulary yet choose your words carefully. With acute powers of observation, writing is an attractive career for you, and you have the skill and dedication to be very successful. You also have an innate sense of rhythm and dexterity so could well be a gifted musician. In your intimate relationship you settle down, but need intellectual stimulation and variety to keep your love alive. At times you read too much into things and can be wary of showing your deeper emotions, much to the frustration of your partner. Twitter was invented just for you!

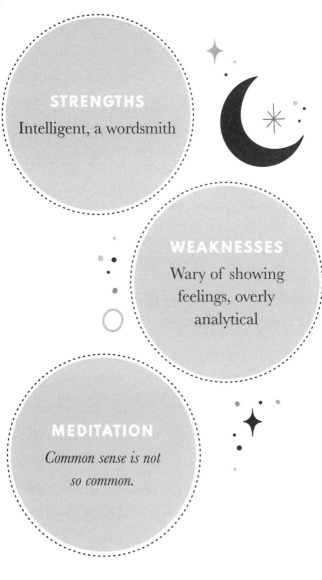

STRENGTHS

Intelligent, a wordsmith

WEAKNESSES

Wary of showing feelings, overly analytical

MEDITATION

Common sense is not so common.

31 December

*Y*ou are a determined and ambitious person, in tune with your emotions, with the added ability to touch the public's mood. You are both shrewd at business and thoughtful, and have a practical, hands-on approach to helping people with their problems. Your organizational skills are impressive and as you get older you spend time using your talents in charitable work. Emotionally you are vulnerable, and are nostalgic for your childhood. Your weakness is over-sensitivity and you take any criticism personally. You have a keen intellect and an excellent memory, perfect for a career in acting or writing. Relationships are crucial for you and you long to create a traditional family life. With your connection to your internal rhythm, drumming would be a brilliantly therapeutic and enjoyable activity.

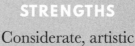

STRENGTHS
Considerate, artistic

WEAKNESSES
Emotionally naive,
sensitive to criticism

MEDITATION
*It is easier to be wise for
others than for ourselves.*

1 January

*Y*ou are a person with initiative and a tremendous drive to succeed. Intensely ambitious, you never stop creating and overcoming challenges. Highly competitive and focused, you have the attributes of an athlete or business tycoon, and you are quite willing to undertake the rigorous training needed to get to the top. You surround yourself with the trappings of success; the right car and home are important to you as you feel they prove your worth. You can be blind to others' feelings, and at times you ride roughshod over weaker opponents; you are also a poor loser. Your lover needs to be someone you are proud of and, once you are sure that they admire you too, you will be a devoted partner. Your energy needs to be released through a tough physical workout at the gym.

STRENGTHS
Motivated, energetic

WEAKNESSES
Intimidating,
a bad loser

MEDITATION
*Years teach us more
than books.*

2 January

*Y*ou are a friendly and reliable person with a great deal of common sense. Ever the realist, you know and appreciate the material world and have excellent organizational skills. Budgeting is your forte; you can be frugal when needed, and have a good eye for a bargain. With a deep love of all things that combine beauty and usefulness, you would make a superb architect or furniture designer. The role of financial manager would also suit you. You can be controlling and rigid in your outlook and are thrown off track when people don't follow the rules. You are a sensual lover, and once committed, are loyal and faithful. Learning to be flexible is your biggest challenge. With your love of nature and artistic colour sense, gardening is the ideal hobby.

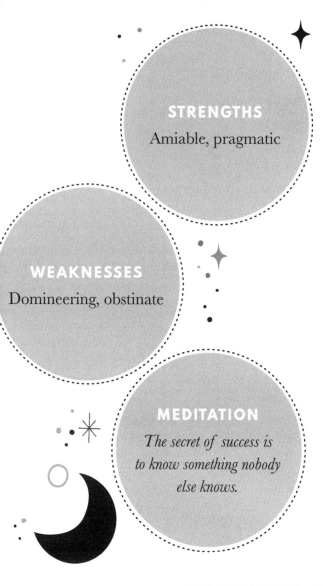

STRENGTHS
Amiable, pragmatic

WEAKNESSES
Domineering, obstinate

MEDITATION
*The secret of success is
to know something nobody
else knows.*

3 January

*Y*ou are a highly intelligent person who loves to talk and is always learning new things. You appear conventional and serious until you relax, when you display a silly and surreal sense of humour. As a gifted communicator whose opinions carry weight, careers as varied as a minister or a political satirist are suitable. With your ready wit you attract friends of all ages and people just adore being in your company. You love playing practical jokes on friends, but can't bear to be laughed at yourself. You are very adaptable and keep up with the latest trends, especially gadgets that aid communication. Your relationships are diverse but the person who sees through your many masks and captures your heart is for keeps. Fancy dress parties allow you to indulge your fun side and entertain others.

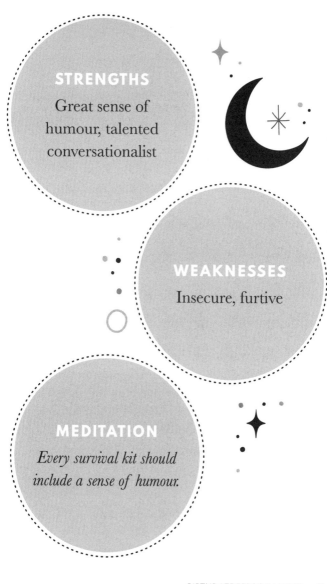

STRENGTHS

Great sense of humour, talented conversationalist

WEAKNESSES

Insecure, furtive

MEDITATION

Every survival kit should include a sense of humour.

4 January

*Y*ou are a caring and kind person who is polite, courteous and well-mannered. You are protective and considerate of people's feelings both at home and at work. As such you are suited to being in a leadership position where taking care of others is the priority and you make an excellent parent. You are a great organizer and capable of paying thorough attention to detail. Your family is important to you and you can be faced with making a choice between home life and your career. Having a home-based business would be an ideal solution. Your relationship keeps you stable and you do need to be needed. You can suffer extreme mood swings and get caught in depression. Activities such as sailing or swimming give you the peace and connection with your inner self that are good for your mind and soul.

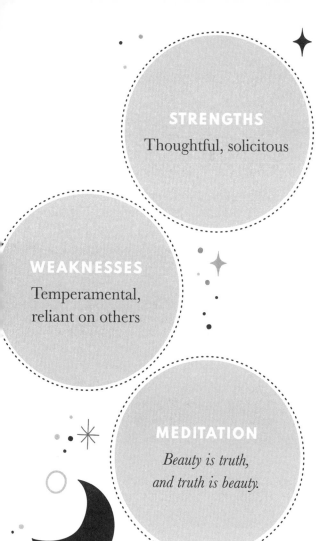

STRENGTHS
Thoughtful, solicitous

WEAKNESSES
Temperamental,
reliant on others

MEDITATION
*Beauty is truth,
and truth is beauty.*

5 January

*Y*ou are a supremely self-confident and creative person. Your aspiration is to be at the top, and you will dedicate your life to achieving just that. There is something of the star about you and you revel in being in the spotlight. Although you work hard you also have time to laugh and play too, which endears you to others. Your enthusiasm and warm-heartedness, added to your desire to make the world a better place, make you a wonderful fundraiser for charity. You are cautious when making decisions, especially those that involve money. A weakness is that you can be too controlling and not allow others to show initiative. When you fall in love it tends to be forever and you are a loyal and passionate partner. Playing children's games is a wonderful way for you to show your silly side.

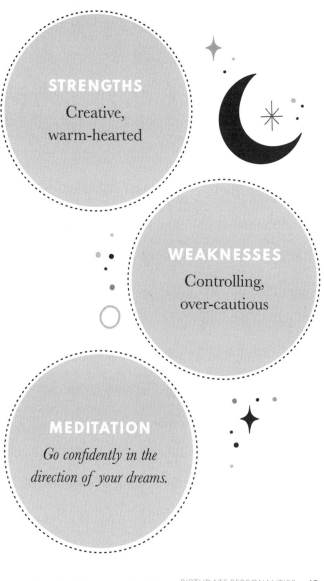

STRENGTHS
Creative,
warm-hearted

WEAKNESSES
Controlling,
over-cautious

MEDITATION
Go confidently in the
direction of your dreams.

6 January

*Y*ou are a reserved and gentle person with a talent for finding the right turn of phrase. With a deep love of the spoken word you are articulate and your humour can be hilarious. You are logical and methodical, and get immense satisfaction from following routines. You make a superb editor and are constantly correcting yourself, but also correcting others. Learning to overlook people's mistakes is a lifelong lesson. People respect you for your achievements and your success is built on a solid foundation of hard work. You tend to avoid risks and can't bear to make mistakes. Your relationships are enduring, but you need your partner to be youthful in outlook, or you will stray. Worrying is your weakness and aromatherapy massage is virtually essential to help you unwind.

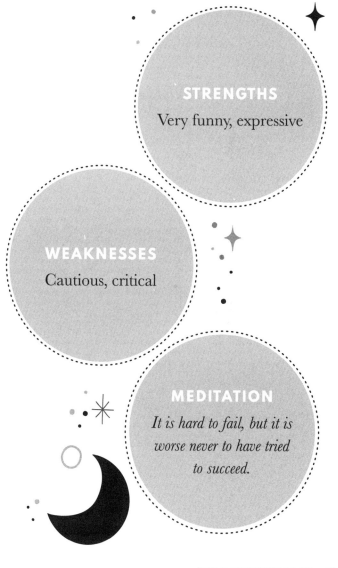

STRENGTHS
Very funny, expressive

WEAKNESSES
Cautious, critical

MEDITATION
It is hard to fail, but it is worse never to have tried to succeed.

7 January

Y ou are a refined and graceful person with immense style and elegance. You are socially adept and know how to play your cards right so you succeed in business. There is a strong sense of purpose in your life – you know where you are going and work steadily to get there. You are able to surround yourself with the most influential people who can advance your career. The worlds of fashion, architecture and finance all have appeal for you. At times you plan too strategically and lack spontaneity. You want people to like you, so you find it hard to say no, which can get you into trouble. You are an appreciative lover and a delightful companion. You can be combative under your peaceful exterior, so sports such as rally driving or fencing are immensely satisfying.

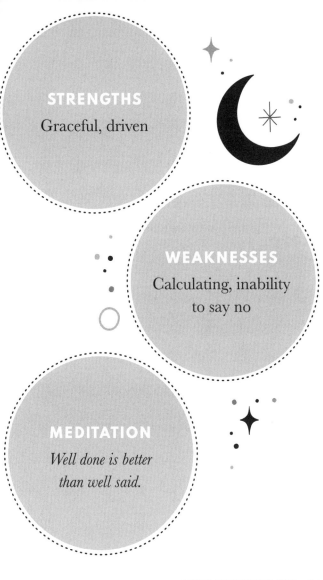

STRENGTHS
Graceful, driven

WEAKNESSES
Calculating, inability
to say no

MEDITATION
*Well done is better
than well said.*

8 January

You are a sensual and magnetic person with a powerful presence. With your penetrating mind and high intelligence you work effectively and laboriously to succeed in the commercial world. Money, and the ease of mind it gives you, is all-important. As a result of your success you can become suspicious of others' motives. You have a strength of character that helps you get through the tough times in your life. Although you are emotionally reserved you have enormous compassion for your fellow man, and you are well qualified to work on regeneration projects. When stressed you can become bogged down in pessimism. A solid relationship gives you much-needed emotional security and you are fiercely protective of your family. A frivolous night out with your friends is a great way to let your hair down.

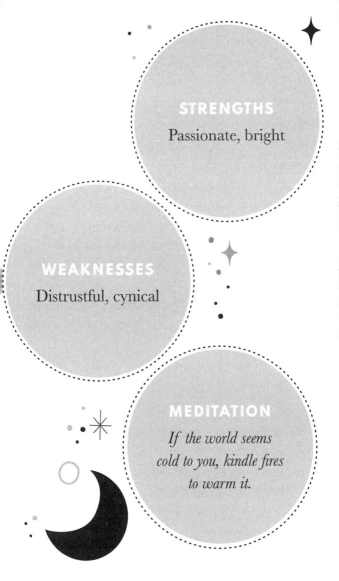

STRENGTHS
Passionate, bright

WEAKNESSES
Distrustful, cynical

MEDITATION
If the world seems cold to you, kindle fires to warm it.

9 January

*Y*ou are a buoyant and optimistic person who can also be deadly serious; a combination that is disarming and enigmatic. You love being in a position of authority, are extremely ambitious and enjoy getting older as people treat you with more respect. You are open-minded, love exploring fresh fields and expanding your circle of influence, often travelling overseas with your work. Since knowledge is so important to you, your ideal role is that of mentor or educator. The legal profession, or even the constantly evolving world of the internet, may also beckon. Ever restless and needing constant change and stimulus, it's not easy for you to settle down with just one person or career. You are a charming lover, easy-going and fun to be with. As you love one-to-one combat, a game of snooker or squash is your ideal workout.

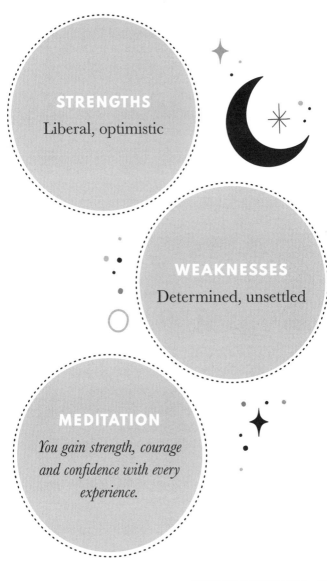

STRENGTHS
Liberal, optimistic

WEAKNESSES
Determined, unsettled

MEDITATION
You gain strength, courage and confidence with every experience.

10 January

*Y*ou are a conscientious and caring person who is a true professional. A superb planner and indefatigable worker, you usually achieve success early in life. One problem is that you tend to take on too much and suffer from the weight of competing demands on your time. Learning to trust and delegate is a big lesson for you. You love anything classic, well-made and stylish and architecture, furniture design and antiques are all areas of interest to you. In relationships you tend to hold back until you're one hundred per cent sure, then you commit whole heartedly. You're the one in charge and will do everything in your power to protect your loved ones. Behind the scenes you reveal your sensuality and often bawdy sense of humour. A good belly laugh does you the world of good.

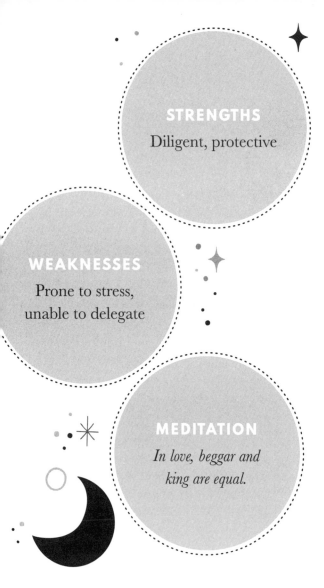

STRENGTHS
Diligent, protective

WEAKNESSES
Prone to stress,
unable to delegate

MEDITATION
*In love, beggar and
king are equal.*

11 January

*Y*ou are a friendly and sociable person who is also self-contained and independent. You have a logical mind and a clear perception of events; you can be very objective about things. You are a gifted organizer and forward planner and you have a love of order, but also of change. Ideally you can bridge the old with the new but at times you struggle when you have to choose between tradition and innovation. You need to be in control, to be the authority and can dig your heels in if someone challenges you. This attitude comes from deeper feelings of insecurity which you tend to cover up. You are attracted to unusual types, and your relationships tend to be unconventional, though a part of you yearns for security. Being out in the fresh air suits you, so take time off walking in wide open spaces.

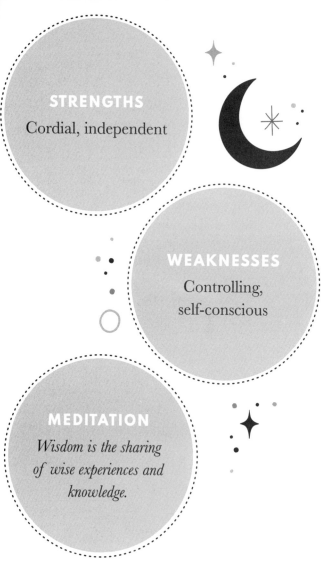

STRENGTHS
Cordial, independent

WEAKNESSES
Controlling,
self-conscious

MEDITATION
*Wisdom is the sharing
of wise experiences and
knowledge.*

12 January

You are a dreamy and sensitive person who also desires material success. Outwardly you come across as business-like and professional, in control of your emotions, but scratch the surface and you are a real softy. Artistic and prepared to work long and hard, you can establish an excellent career for yourself in theatre, art or creative writing. Your sensitivity also makes you a compassionate counsellor as you are willing to help people on a practical level. Your weakness is that you can take on others' emotional burdens and then lose confidence in yourself. In love you are tender-hearted and devoted to your beloved. However, you can become very needy and dependent. Singing opens your heart, and an evening at a karaoke bar is terrific fun for you and allows you to gain confidence in yourself.

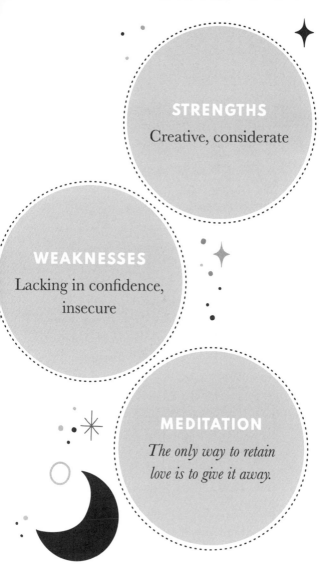

STRENGTHS
Creative, considerate

WEAKNESSES
Lacking in confidence,
insecure

MEDITATION
*The only way to retain
love is to give it away.*

13 January

*Y*ou are a tough yet tender person with a practical, no-nonsense approach to life. You are in touch with your emotions and self-aware, and enjoy spending a great deal of time alone. Some might say you are too self-absorbed. Looking good and feeling good are important to you as you are not overly robust. You have a close relationship with your family and often keep in contact with childhood friends. Work is important and you take pride in maintaining a high standard in all that you do. You are happiest working in established companies. You get the best from people as you truly listen to them and empathize. In relationships you are often attracted to an older partner. You will commit early as you need to find your 'other half'. Time spent in nature, especially in forests, really boosts your energy.

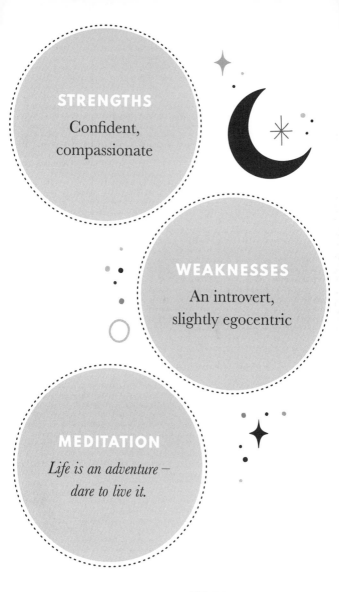

STRENGTHS

Confident,
compassionate

WEAKNESSES

An introvert,
slightly egocentric

MEDITATION

*Life is an adventure —
dare to live it.*

14 January

*Y*ou are a vibrant and forceful person whose warmth and radiance are felt by all who meet you. A natural leader, you are cut out for high-flying business roles. You are a polished professional and had big plans for success from an early age. As you are ambitious, you are happiest when juggling a variety of responsibilities. Your reputation matters to you and you take care to keep your personal life private. Although you appear supremely confident there is always a voice of self-doubt inside. At times you can come across as vain and self-centred, but people forgive you since you really do know how to show the way and have fun. A naturally amorous and expressive lover, you devote yourself to your partner and family. Charades is a great game for you and your friends.

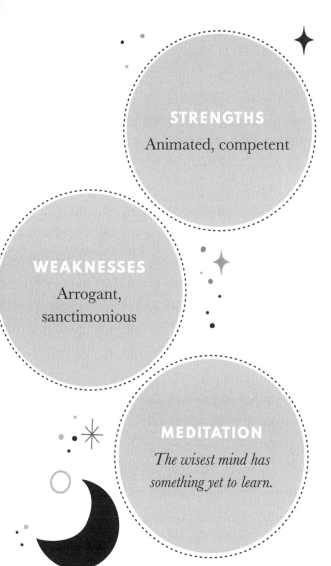

STRENGTHS
Animated, competent

WEAKNESSES
Arrogant, sanctimonious

MEDITATION
The wisest mind has something yet to learn.

15 January

*Y*ou are a deeply caring person with a strong work ethic. You work tirelessly on behalf of others, wanting to serve and help them in a practical way. With a clear, logical mind, your communication skills are superb, and you consider precisely what you want to say. It is rare that you get caught off guard. You make a brilliant orator and writer especially on subjects involving a lot of research. When upset you can be cranky and over-fastidious. A serious student, you love learning and do so all your life. You choose friends carefully and they get to know the softer, more sentimental side of you. In relationships you are at first cool and emotionally reserved; once you feel safe you become a thoughtful and romantic lover. Pruning the garden is an ideal way to unwind.

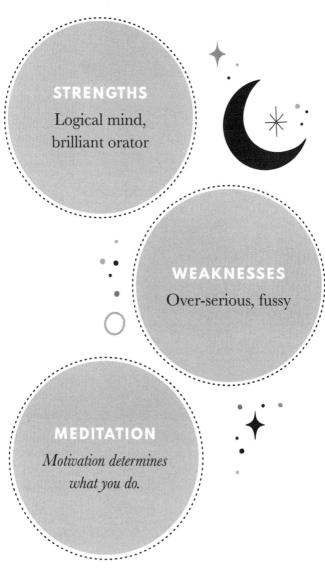

STRENGTHS

Logical mind,
brilliant orator

WEAKNESSES

Over-serious, fussy

MEDITATION

*Motivation determines
what you do.*

16 January

*Y*ou are a popular and socially aware person with an alluring aura. You mix in influential circles and have many friends in high places. A canny business mind, combined with a dry wit, gives you an advantage in the world of commerce. Immensely stylish, you dress well with a chic, understated look, and you apply your good taste to everything you own. Interior design and fashion are just two possible careers. You are intensely pragmatic, but can sometimes get trapped in negative thinking and become cynical. Partnership is essential for you, whether personal or business, as you need someone to bounce ideas off. A born romantic, you court your lover and take great pleasure in buying them gifts. An art exhibition is the perfect romantic and cultural experience for you.

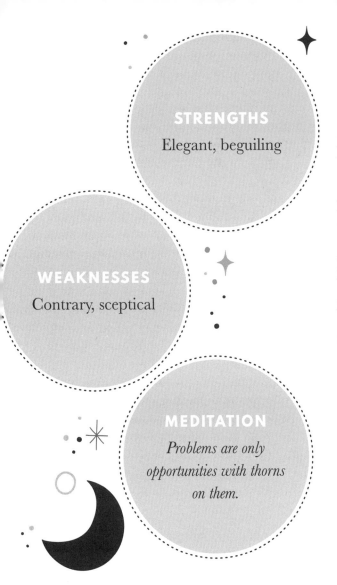

STRENGTHS

Elegant, beguiling

WEAKNESSES

Contrary, sceptical

MEDITATION

Problems are only opportunities with thorns on them.

17 January

*Y*ou are an enigmatic and passionately dedicated person with a tough inner core. Tenacious and ambitious, you apply yourself to your career and will sacrifice personal pleasures to attain your goals. Keen to understand yourself and human emotions, you are attracted to the fields of psychology and psychiatry. In your youth you can be self-conscious and shy, but as you get older you become more self-assured and confident. You are a trustworthy and loyal friend and have a wicked sense of humour. You live by a high moral code and can impose your standards on others, demanding that they behave in a certain way. In relationships, you need a faithful partner as you can be jealous and possessive. To keep your marriage alive, an expensive dinner and a night out at a hotel with your beloved has the thrill you seek.

STRENGTHS
Mysterious, comical

WEAKNESSES
Moralistic, with a jealous streak

MEDITATION
Great effort springs naturally from a great attitude.

18 January

*Y*ou are a big-hearted, extravagant and hard-working person. A builder and adventurer, you are on a quest to discover yourself and the world. You never cease from garnering knowledge and distilling it into your own unique brand of wisdom. Not suited to be an underling, you thrive when self-employed. A shrewd gambler, your intuition is strong, so you make calculated risks and solid investments. Your business interests are varied and could encompass a travel company, horse riding school, or running a casino. A problem you have is wasting nervous energy, always seeking new ventures. Love affairs are many; it's later in life that you settle down with your intellectual equal. You are a generous partner and shower your lover with gifts. A sporty type, you love being outdoors, so running or rowing is excellent.

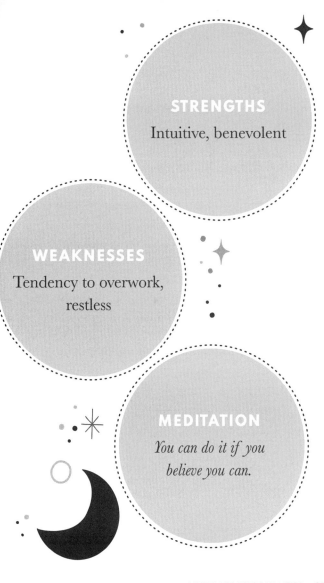

STRENGTHS

Intuitive, benevolent

WEAKNESSES

Tendency to overwork,
restless

MEDITATION

*You can do it if you
believe you can.*

19 January

*Y*ou are a helpful and trustworthy person that others depend upon. Intensely ambitious, you make a sure and steady climb to the top. Always working, you need material security and recognition for your accomplishments. Status really matters to you. There are times when you can get overwhelmed with the monumental tasks you have set yourself, so it is vital to make time to be with friends in your busy schedule. Remember, it can be lonely at the top. A lover of tradition, you have a strong set of values and marriage suits you. Your partner gives you much-needed balance and you are attracted to an emotional person who just adores you. You maintain a well-organized household and strive to ensure that everyone feels secure. Letting your hair down with some light-hearted fun will lighten your load.

STRENGTHS
Reliable, determined

WEAKNESSES
Unable to relax,
uptight

MEDITATION
*The more alternatives, the
more difficult the choice.*

20 January

*Y*ou are a practical and peaceful person with good old-fashioned traditional values. You are patient and well-disciplined and always stay the course. Physically and emotionally you improve with age and assume the role of the elder with immense style and grace. You work hard to achieve material success as it buys you the home and the security you need. It often takes early success, however, to give you the self-confidence to meet challenges. Your weakness is that you can be too possessive of things and people and become reliant on the same familiar routines. You are a trustworthy and generous friend and love to invite people over for dinner parties. Your relationship means a great deal to you and you tend to meet your life partner at an early age. A treat that helps loosen you up is an aromatherapy massage – worth every penny.

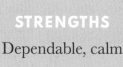

STRENGTHS
Dependable, calm

WEAKNESSES
Controlling, afraid
of change

MEDITATION
*You are the master
of your fate; you are the
captain of your soul.*

Going
DEEPER

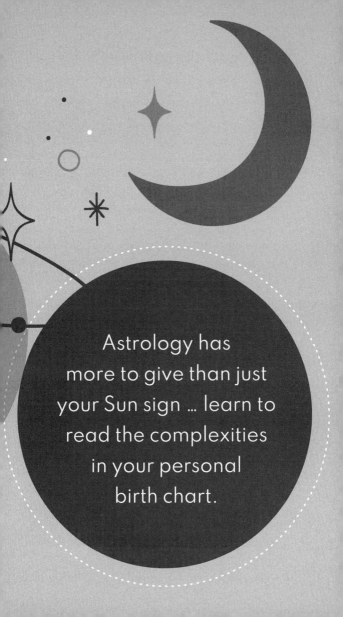

Astrology has more to give than just your Sun sign ... learn to read the complexities in your personal birth chart.

Your personal birth chart

*U*nderstanding your Sun sign is an essential part of astrology, but it's the tip of the iceberg. To take your astrological wisdom to the next level, you'll need a copy of your unique birth chart – a map of the heavens for the precise moment you were born. You can find your birth chart at the Free Horoscopes link at: www.astro.com.

ASTROLOGICAL SYNTHESIS

When you first explore your chart you'll find that as well as a Sun sign, you also have a Moon sign, plus a Mercury, Venus, Mars, Jupiter, Saturn, Neptune, Uranus and Pluto sign – and that they all mean something different. Then there's astrological houses to consider, ruling planets and Rising signs, aspects and element types – all of which you will learn more about in the birth chart section on pages 112–115.

The art to astrology is in synthesising all this intriguing information to paint a picture of someone's character, layer by layer. Now that you understand your Capricorn Sun personality better, it's time to go deeper, and to look at the next layer – your Moon sign. To find your own Moon sign go to pages 104–111.

THE MOON'S INFLUENCE

After the Sun, your Moon sign is the second biggest astrological influence in your birth chart. It describes your emotional nature – your feelings, instincts and moods and how you respond to different sorts of people and situations. By blending your outer, Capricorn Sun character with your inner, emotional, Moon sign, you'll get a much more balanced picture. If you don't feel that you're 100% Capricorn, your Moon sign will probably explain why!

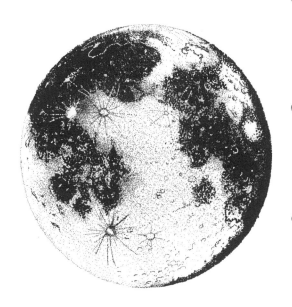

Capricorn with Moon signs

CAPRICORN SUN/**ARIES MOON**

You're a formidable mix of ambition, passion and strength. You need financial stability and to have a secure career path with something to work towards. Goal-oriented and methodical, you have the drive to succeed and want to have something to show for it. Emotionally you are passionate, with a quick temper but you're more demonstrative than an out-and-out Capricorn. Your Mars/Saturn combination imbues you with the will to succeed, and you enjoy being challenged or told that you won't be able to do something, just so you can prove them wrong! You need a partner you can relax with, someone who accepts you for who you are. Your initial reactions to problems will be to rush in aggressively, but what you really need is to be able to talk to someone close about your woes instead of expecting a fight.

CAPRICORN SUN/**TAURUS MOON**

You're a double-Earth person, patient, reliable, loyal and strong. You believe in what you can see, hear and touch, and making money and having a secure home and family base will be very important to you. You're a traditionalist at heart and work very hard to make a comfortable life yourself and your loved ones. It's hard to change your mind once you have made a decision, but a little more flexibility would serve you well. You tend to fixate on one outcome when there are probably more options than you wish to take on board. You're happiest with a stable, partnership with someone who'd rather build on what they have than over-react to the slightest change in circumstance – though a little spontaneity wouldn't go amiss!

CAPRICORN SUN/**GEMINI MOON**

 You have a brilliant business mind and a knack for knowing where to invest your time and money. You're as good with details as you are at looking at the whole picture from a pragmatic point of view. Tenacious but restless, you throw yourself into work, absorbing information at a tremendous rate, but because you invest so much mental energy into everything you do, it's important you take regular breaks. You probably have an incredible memory and are as interested in fashion and social media as you are in law or politics. Your sunnier Mercury-ruled Moon is at odds with your more reflective Saturn-ruled Sun, and you probably leap from one extreme to the other, emotionally. You work best with a partner who is on the same level intellectually, as you need someone smart and stimulating to keep you interested.

CAPRICORN SUN/**CANCER MOON**

 Capricorn and Cancer are opposite signs of the zodiac, which means you were born at a full Moon. You have an astute business sense, with excellent money-making potential as your Capricorn Sun is goal-oriented and good with money. Your Cancer Moon is also tenacious and concerned with security. Your lesson is to learn to balance your home and family life with your career aspirations as both are equally as important to you. Perhaps working from home or in a partnership with your relatives would work well for you. You are a deeply sensitive person, much more than people realise and you need a safe retreat from the outside world. You may be a hard-headed, well respected executive by day, but at night you're likely to be a homebody, happy with a home-cooked meal and to be cuddled up with loved ones on the sofa.

CAPRICORN SUN/**LEO MOON**

 You're a popular and natural leader with an air of authority that means people instinctively turn to you for advice. You have inner reserves of energy and strong will power, helping you tackle any challenges on your path. Enjoying being in the spotlight, you'd work best when you're in the public eye, perhaps as a politician, entertainer or public relations officer. You need to be careful that you don't become a workaholic as you also have a very creative side. You may excel at dancing, acting, or be a skilled artist or crafter. You will be more sociable and outgoing than most Capricorns and will probably have a large circle of friends. Your ideal partner would be someone who sees through your tough, Capricorn shell to the approval-seeking person inside, and can give you heaps of encouragement to be yourself.

CAPRICORN SUN/**VIRGO MOON**

You're an extremely well-organised person – neat, meticulous and analytical – with an aptitude for research, analysis and detailed work. You can become so concentrated on what you're doing that you forget the outside world. You like to plan things carefully so prefer to have a set routine and feel calm when you know exactly where you'll be going and what you'll be doing. Observant and critical, you're an excellent problem solver with a rational and responsible mind. You're not keen on attention and can be quite shy but a supportive, loving partner will still be very important to you. Virgo Moon people are kind and helpful and like to feel useful. You probably need to make time to relax as you'll find it hard to switch off your perfectionism.

CAPRICORN SUN/**LIBRA MOON**

You're a level-headed, sociable person, who usually has a good work/life balance. Other people's opinions really matter to you, as you dislike conflict and want to make everyone happy. Loved ones turn to you for advice because they know you to be impartial and wise with excellent judgement. And your thoughtful Capricorn Sun means you're likely to be sensible and shrewd with money. Libra Moon people have a lot of love to give, and looking for the right person will take priority. You're happiest in a partnership, whether that's romantic or a business relationship, and the other person's views will be almost as important as your own. Conflict makes you uneasy and you'll often agree with people just to avoid an uncomfortable situation. But when you do make your point it's usually sensible, nuanced and wise.

CAPRICORN SUN/**SCORPIO MOON**

 Your responsible Saturn-ruled Sun and ardent Pluto-ruled Scorpio Moon gives you a powerful and very capable character. You'll be ambitious and shrewd with the desire to land a top job. You're very observant of the people around you, and although you notice everything, you usually keep this information to yourself. You're good with money and have a sixth sense about what makes a good investment. You're probably cautious and a little shy, even though you have an intensely emotional inner nature. You're discriminating in love and seek a partner who'll keep you on your toes, and are usually happy to stay single if the right person hasn't come along. But if you do meet someone compatible, they'll need to be completely trustworthy as this is a vital requirement for a Scorpio Moon person.

CAPRICORN SUN/**SAGITTARIUS MOON**

 You may be a reserved person, but you have an excellent sense of humour. Behind your professional, worldly exterior lies a warm, philosophical and deep-thinking soul. You love to travel and meet people from different cultures, and are fascinated by what others believe in and find important. Competitive and enthusiastic, you love a challenge, and your success at work will be well documented. In relationships you look for an open-minded and confident person who'll appreciate your need for freedom. Physical attraction is only a small part of what draws you to another person, as you need intellectual compatibility first and foremost. You like time alone to make new discoveries, but you also like to share what you've learned with a soulmate.

CAPRICORN SUN/**CAPRICORN MOON**

 You are probably quite a solemn person, quiet and wise. But you are observant, clever and extremely well organised. You work well on your own and can see your way through even the most challenging of circumstances. You have a clear vision of what you want to achieve and how you're going to get there, and you can be something of a workaholic. But a secure loving relationship can mellow your 'tough love' attitude to life, and encouragement from loved ones gives you the confidence to be loved for who you really are – rather than the controlled, responsible person you are in public. As a double-Earth Sun and Moon person you are encouraged to explore your creative side as this could prove to be an extremely therapeutic way of expressing any locked-up feelings.

CAPRICORN SUN/**AQUARIUS MOON**

An extremely knowledgeable person, you work very hard to achieve your aims. Humanitarian and political, you wish to connect with people on a grand scale and you'll work towards creating a better planet for everyone. You have an active social life and probably belong to many different clubs and organisations, and may have a reputation for your off-beat sense of style. You have a quirky, slightly rebellious side, which lightens your authoritative Capricorn side considerably, and although your friendships will be vitally important, romantic relationships may be tricky. Your Uranus-ruled emotional side can be changeable and a little detached. You have an unconventional but friendly nature and are devoted to the people you love, though you find conflict disturbing and stay clear of drama.

CAPRICORN SUN/**PISCES MOON**

You're a dedicated and compassionate person, empathic and strong. Your Saturn-Ruled Sun and Neptune-ruled Moon give you great insight into the human condition and you'll probably wish to work in an area where you can help people in trouble. You'd be a trustworthy and wise counsellor and you're a loyal and loving friend. Emotionally you're an idealist, which will probably bring some difficulties in romance as you expect so much from your loved ones. But as you get older you have a more realistic take on love and your Capricorn Sun will temper your vivid imagination to something more realistic and easier to attain. You likely have artistic ability which you should be careful not to ignore, as you're probably much more talented than you even realise.

Birth charts

*L*earning about your Sun and Moon sign opens the gateway into exploring your own birth chart. This snapshot of the skies at the moment of someone's birth is as complex and interesting as the person it represents. Astrologers the world over have been studying their own birth charts and those of people they know, their whole lives and still find something new in them every day. There are many schools of astrology and an inexhaustible list of tools and techniques, but here are the essentials to get you started ...

ZODIAC SIGNS AND PLANETS

These are the keywords for the 12 zodiac signs and the planets associated with them, known as ruling planets.

 ARIES
courageous, bold, aggressive, leading, impulsive

Ruling planet
 MARS
shows where you take action and how you channel your energy

TAURUS

reliable, artistic, practical, stubborn, patient

Ruling planet
VENUS

describes what you value and who and what you love

GEMINI

clever, friendly, superficial, versatile

Ruling planet
MERCURY

represents how your mind works and how you communicate

CANCER

emotional, nurturing, defensive, sensitive

Ruling planet
MOON

describes your emotional needs and how you wish to be nurtured

LEO

confidence, radiant, proud, vain, generous

Ruling planet
SUN

your core personality and character

VIRGO
analytical, organised, meticulous, thrifty

Ruling planet
MERCURY
co-ruler of Gemini and Virgo

LIBRA
fair, indecisive, cooperative, diplomatic

Ruling planet
VENUS
co-ruler of Taurus and Libra

SCORPIO
regenerating, magnetic, obsessive, penetrating

Ruling planet
PLUTO
deep transformation, endings and beginnings

SAGITTARIUS
optimistic, visionary, expansive, blunt, generous

Ruling planet
JUPITER
travel, education and faith in a higher power

CAPRICORN

ambitious, responsible, cautious, conventional

Ruling planet
SATURN

your ambitions, work ethic and restrictions

AQUARIUS

unconventional, independent, erratic, unpredictable

Ruling planet
URANUS

where you rebel or innovate

PISCES

dreamy, chaotic, compassionate, imaginative, idealistic

Ruling planet
NEPTUNE

your unconscious, and where you let things go

The 12 houses

Birth charts are divided into 12 sections, known as houses, each relating to different areas of life as follows:

FIRST HOUSE
associated with *Aries*
Identity – how you appear to others and your initial response to challenges.

SECOND HOUSE
associated with *Taurus*
How you make and spend money, your talents, skills and how you value yourself.

THIRD HOUSE
associated with *Gemini*
Siblings, neighbours, communication and short distance travel.

FOURTH HOUSE
associated with *Cancer*
Home, family, your mother, roots and the past.

FIFTH HOUSE
associated with *Leo*
Love affairs, romance, creativity, gambling and children.

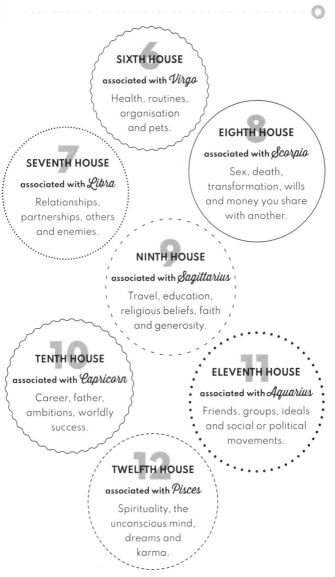

SIXTH HOUSE

associated with *Virgo*

Health, routines, organisation and pets.

EIGHTH HOUSE

associated with *Scorpio*

Sex, death, transformation, wills and money you share with another.

SEVENTH HOUSE

associated with *Libra*

Relationships, partnerships, others and enemies.

NINTH HOUSE

associated with *Sagittarius*

Travel, education, religious beliefs, faith and generosity.

TENTH HOUSE

associated with *Capricorn*

Career, father, ambitions, worldly success.

ELEVENTH HOUSE

associated with *Aquarius*

Friends, groups, ideals and social or political movements.

TWELFTH HOUSE

associated with *Pisces*

Spirituality, the unconscious mind, dreams and karma.

THE ELEMENTS

Each zodiac sign belongs to one of the four elements – Earth, Air, Fire and Water – and these share similar characteristics.

EARTH

Taurus, Virgo, Capricorn

Earth signs are practical, trustworthy, thorough and logical.

AIR

Gemini, Libra, Aquarius

Air signs are clever, flighty, intellectual and charming.

FIRE

Aries, Leo, Sagittarius

Fire signs are active, creative, warm, spontaneous, innovators.

WATER

Cancer, Scorpio, Pisces

Water signs are sensitive, empathic, dramatic and caring.

PLANETARY ASPECTS

The aspects are geometric patterns formed by the planets and represent different types of energy. They are usually shown in two ways - in a separate grid or aspect grid and as the criss-crossing lines on the chart itself. There are oodles of different aspect patterns but to keep things simple we'll just be working with four: conjunctions, squares, oppositions and trines.

CONJUNCTION

0 degrees apart
intensifying

SQUARE

90 degrees apart
challenging

OPPOSITION

180 degrees apart
polarising

TRINE

120 degrees apart
harmonising

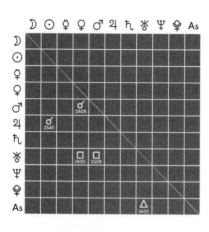

Planetary
aspects for
Hannah's
chart

HOUSES AND RISING SIGN

Each chart is a 360° circle, divided into 12 segments known as the houses (see pages 116–117 for house interpretations). The most important point in a birth chart is known as the Rising sign, which shows the zodiac sign on the Eastern horizon for the moment you were born. This is usually marked as ASC or AS on the chart drawing. This is the position from where the other houses and zodiac signs are drawn in a counter-clockwise direction. The Rising sign is always on the dividing line of the first house - the house associated with the self, how you appear to others, and the lens through which you view the world.

CHART RULER: The planetary ruler of a person's Rising zodiac sign is always a key player in unlocking a birth chart and obtaining a deeper understanding of it.

A SIMPLE BIRTH CHART INTERPRETATION FOR A CAPRICORN SUN PERSON

BIRTH CHART FOR HANNAH, BORN 18 JANUARY 1985 IN HOLYHEAD, UK.

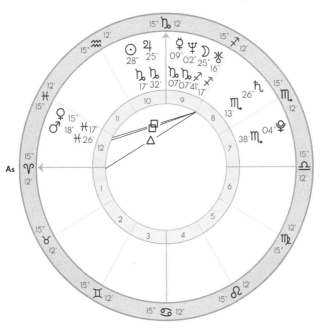

THE POSITION OF THE PLANETS: Hannah has Aries Rising. The Sun is in Capricorn, the Moon's in Sagittarius, Mercury is in Capricorn, Venus and Mars are positioned in Pisces, Jupiter's in Capricorn, Saturn sits in Scorpio, Uranus is in Sagittarius, Neptune's in Capricorn and

Pluto occupies Scorpio. Also note the house positions that the planets are in.

INTERPRETATION BASICS

How do you begin to put all these signs and symbols together? It's usually best to begin with the Sun, Rising sign (As), and then to examine the condition of the Moon sign.

SUN, MOON, RISING SIGN AND CHART RULER: Hannah's Sun (creativity/core personality) was positioned inside ambitious, responsible Capricorn when she was born, and it was in the tenth house (work/public image). As Jupiter, the planet of luck and expansion, is conjunct (strengthening) the Sun, this is a solidly fortunate placement for Hannah, indicating a job or work in public life that opens many opportunities for growth and travel – and gives her the ability to make a mark on her chosen profession.

Hannah's Moon (emotions/feelings/reactions) is in cheerful, adventurous Sagittarius, meaning that emotionally she is idealistic and philosophical, and needs plenty of room to express herself. She probably needs to escape from mundane routines sometimes and explore life's bigger themes.

Hannah has Aries Rising sign (As), which places all the signs in her chart in the houses they rule. For example, Aries in the first, Taurus in the second, and so on. This is known as a 'natural chart', as the signs and houses are a natural fit. This can make the interpretation a little less complicated, but the birth chart's meaning still depends on the planets' positions, signs and angles, taken as a whole.

With Hannah's pioneering, headstrong Aries Rising sign (As), she deals with new situations head-on and likes to win. Her chart ruler is Mars (energetic/impulsive), which is situated in the twelfth house (subconscious/psychic) in nebulous Pisces. This means Hannah will take on the world in an extremely imaginative and energetic way. Mars is a straightforward Fire sign and Pisces likes to take a back seat, and to hide from the world, so she'll likely be an intriguing mixture of full-on exuberance with a compassionate, visionary approach.

Hannah's Venus (relationships/talents) is also conjunct (strengthening) her Mars chart ruler, which is also in empathic Pisces, which could indicate artistic or creative abilities. Perhaps she uses music, art or writing as a shield (Mars) or way of coping with life's ups and downs.

OTHER PLANETS: Hannah's Mercury (communication) is in Capricorn (determination/ambition) – residing in her ninth house (philosophy/freedom and knowledge) implying enjoyment of debate, a philosophical outlook and a willingness to improve.

Saturn (restriction/hard work) sits in intense Scorpio in the eighth house (shared resources/mysteries), perhaps indicating money issues with other people, or even a secretive approach to her finances. Uranus (change/innovation) is in Sagittarius (travel/

freedom) which has an inventive, restless flavour, probably encouraging Hannah to try as many different experiences as possible.

Poetic, boundary-free Neptune resides in worldly Capricorn, suggesting artistic ambition, or a charitable worldview, and in the ninth house of travel, would make her an effective ambassador for people in crisis. Hannah's Pluto (endings/resources) in Scorpio is strong in its own sign and house, and may suggest dramatic and dynamic relationships.

ADDING IN THE PLANETARY ASPECTS

Let's take a brief look at the strongest aspects – the ones with the most exact angles or 'orbs' to the planetary degrees (the numbers next to the planets).

SUN CONJUNCT JUPITER: Hannah's core personality (Sun) is positive and carefree (Jupiter), indicating someone who can achieve anything she sets her mind to (conjunction).

VENUS CONJUNCT MARS: Hannah's relationships and talents (Venus) receive a powerful boost (conjunction) when she takes action, or puts herself forward and takes command (Mars).

VENUS AND MARS SQUARE URANUS: Hannah has energetic, dynamic (Mars) relationships (Venus) and when she finds herself confronted (square) with change (Uranus) she has to find compromises that work for all parties.

URANUS TRINE RISING SIGN (AS): Hannah has an erratic but inventive (Uranus) approach to dealing with any challenge life throws at her (Rising sign/As) and this usually works in her favour (trine).

YOUR JOB AS AN ASTROLOGER

The interpretation above is simplified to help you understand some of the nuts and bolts of interpretation. There are almost as many techniques and tools for analysing birth charts as there are people!

Remember when you're putting the whole thing together that astrology doesn't show negatives or positives. The planets represent potential and opportunities, rather than definitions set in stone. It's your job as an astrologer to use the planets' wisdom to blend and synthesise those energies to create the picture of a whole person.

Going deeper

To see your own birth chart visit: www.astro.com and click the Free Horoscopes link and then enter your birth information. If you don't know what time you were born, put in 12.00pm. Your Rising sign and the houses might not be right, but the planets will be in the correct zodiac signs and the aspects will be accurate.

Further reading and credits

WWW.ASTRO.COM

This amazing astrological resource is extremely popular with both experienced and beginner astrologers. It's free to sign up and obtain your birth chart and personalised daily horoscopes.

BOOKS

PARKER'S ASTROLOGY by Derek and Julia Parker (Dorling Kindersley)

THE LITTLE BOOK OF ASTROLOGY by Marion Williamson (Summersdale)

THE BIRTHDAY ORACLE by Pam Carruthers (Arcturus)

THE 12 HOUSES by Howard Sasportas (London School of Astrology)

THE ARKANA DICTIONARY OF ASTROLOGY by Fred Gettings (Penguin)

THE ROUND ART by AJ Mann (Paper Tiger)

THE LUMINARIES by Liz Greene (Weiser)

SUN SIGNS by Linda Goodman (Pan Macmillan)

Marion Williamson is a best-selling astrology author and editor. *The Little Book of Astrology* and *The Little Book of the Zodiac* (Summersdale 2018) consistently feature in Amazon's top 20 astrology books. These were written to encourage beginners to move past Sun signs and delve into what can be a lifetime's study. Marion has been writing about different areas of self-discovery for over 30 years. A former editor of *Prediction* magazine for ten years, Marion had astrology columns in *TVTimes*, *TVEasy*, *Practical Parenting*, *Essentials* and *Anglers Mail* for over ten years. Twitter: @_I_am_astrology

Pam Carruthers is a qualified professional Vedic and Western astrologer and student of *A Course in Miracles*. An experienced Life Coach and Trainer, Pam helps clients discover the hidden patterns that are holding them back in their lives. A consultation with her is a life-enhancing and healing experience. She facilitates a unique transformational workshop 'Healing your Birth Story' based on your birthchart. Based in the UK, Pam has an international clientele.

All images courtesy of Shutterstock and Freepik/ Flaticon.com.

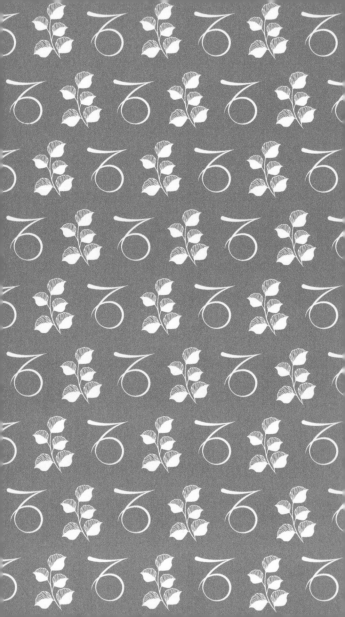